The Scenery of Saviors

poems by

Maria Sebastian

Finishing Line Press
Georgetown, Kentucky

The Scenery of Saviors

I really like human beings who have suffered. They're kinder.

—*Emma Thompson*

Copyright © 2019 by Maria Sebastian
ISBN 978-1-64662-031-9 First Edition
All rights reserved under International and Pan-American Copyright Conventions. No part of this book may be reproduced in any manner whatsoever without written permission from the publisher, except in the case of brief quotations embodied in critical articles and reviews.

ACKNOWLEDGMENTS

The following publications have previously published works that appear in this collection:

"Ode to the House Dress" *Lily Poetry Review*
"I Want to Ask My Mother" *Metonym Literary Journal*
"The Refugee's Ode to Yet" *The Larger Geometry* anthology, San Antonio peaceCENTER Press.
"Morning in the Community College Writing Lab" *About Place*
"She Met a Guy" *The Stirling Spoon*
"A Portrait of Your Boy and Mine" *Mothers Always Write*
"A Mother's Dream (On the Eve of Her Son's First Day of Junior Year)" *The Menteur*
"Is Maria There" and "After a Funeral for a Man in His Twenties" *Owen Wister Review*
"A Good Game" *Hobart Literary Journal*
"Squirrel Hill Tunnel" *White Wall Review*
"I Heard a Woman" was published by *Broad River Review*
"Man Made Art" was published by *The Showbear Family Circus*

Publisher: Leah Maines
Editor: Christen Kincaid
Cover Art: Getty Images / Public Domain
Author Photo: Maria Sebastian
Cover Design: Elizabeth Maines McCleavy

Printed in the USA on acid-free paper.
Order online: www.finishinglinepress.com
also available on amazon.com

Author inquiries and mail orders:
Finishing Line Press
P. O. Box 1626
Georgetown, Kentucky 40324
U. S. A.

Table of Contents

She Met a Guy 1
A Mother's Dream (on the Eve of Her Son's First Day in
    Eleventh Grade) 2
Hope is a Community College Writing Lab 3
A Good Game 4
Today I Am Craving 5
Ode to The House Dress 6
Zaynab in the Community College Writing Lab 7
Firefighter to Grandchild 9
Man Made Art 10
A Refugee's Ode to Yet 11
I Want to Ask My Mother 12
I Heard a Woman 13
Squirrel Hill Tunnel 14
Is Maria There 15
The Wheel 16
Tug of War 18
After Attending a Funeral for a Man in His Twenties 20
A Portrait of Your Boy and Mine 22
Paying My Way Through College 23
To the School Shooter 25
Why I Should Never Be Responsible for Another Living Being .. 27
Another Buffalo Banquet 28
Pre-Caffeine Minutia 30
The Scenery of Saviors 32
Middle Life 33

She Met a Guy

whenever anyone asks
how Mom is at the nursing home
I tell them she met a guy
and they smile and say *how cute*
he makes her laugh I add
lets her beat him at rummy

repeats her stories to strangers
she was in a beauty contest
she didn't smile or she'd have won
she used to decorate all her houses
he even tells me about myself
you could sing before you could talk

you sang that Debbie Boone song
"You Light Up My Life"
you were only four years old
she told him this weeks ago
Chris was once a substitute teacher
Mom introduces him as a Professor of English

what's the difference really
he is a hero of the humanities
complimenting her rhinestone clasp bracelet
the one she wears to meet him
at the card table in the community room
where he hooks her cameo necklace

like a nurse and a best friend and a true love
the last voice she would want to hear
if she could choose a last to hear
a new friend who knows just enough
to validate this version of her
the one she worked all her life to perfect

1

A Mother's Dream (on the Eve of Her Son's First Day in Eleventh Grade)

I can only remember sketches
usually dream of forgetting lunch or water bottles
the first week of school always one giant to-do list
this time I woke half a dozen times
editing his list and mine

in between was a series of chilling clips
dim yellow-lit stairwells cautioning
a twenty-something man quickly casting
shadows across a boiler room hallway
I huddled in a closet with a rifle

I apparently owned or found or stole
then aimed through the cracked doorway
bullet navigating black air in slow motion
bloodying the intruder's bulky Rambo arm
I screamed loud enough to deafen decades

for my son to run the other way
he wasn't even there
scenes pooled in whirls of what now
between that shot and my blazing alarm
I tried to brush it off at the coffeemaker

watched him walk into school like always
just another mother clinging like mortar to brick
I used to feel safe once a bad dream ended
and it was just a dream to me
but each day I send my boy back in

Hope Is a Community College Writing Lab

four tables four tutors four hours per week
I help young writers articulate rocket blasts

today I wait my turn while two teams buzz
students recalling the falling of midnight skies

one ear for each war   I spy nearby   brace
for poetic impact   a ballpoint bullseye

then comes Julie in need of my help
I must tune out   assist with her theme dilemma

—*my professor said hope comes from someplace—
and Dickinson—*

but I want the-brown-man-over-there's theme
how will he establish his purpose   resolve his peace

I want his perception of hope   his song his colors
I want his mother's eyes when not crying

Julie talks at me   I cling to the bass in his voice
I want the whole picture   as Emily certainly would

A Good Game

good game

good game

good game

good game

good game

good game

good game

good game

good game

good game

good game

good game

Today I Am Craving

a walk around a corner
I memorized for no reason
no reason it seemed
the day I waved myself goodbye

in Chicago I believe ah yes
no better feeling than walking alone
with a purpose under doting skyscrapers
through a city so tightly woven

today I am craving possibility
leaping from a brownstone window
in black patent leather roller skates
landing center street all smiles

gliding double yellow lines in a surfer pose
swinging a burnt orange briefcase
sporting hope-rimmed sunglasses
chosen for breakfast with Ms. Angelou

and after skating for miles I'll jump
the Seventh Avenue bus for a bit
watch waitresses wink at commuters
to try their new soul food menu

or delight in new diamond cuff links
for which we know the price and the cost
today I am craving America
a slow motion black and white documentary

Maya and I will meet in Harlem
near the t-shirt tables outside the Apollo
to get a grip on how we might fit in
fashion our way as part of the fabric

Ode to The House Dress

and so even the children of hard-to-like mothers
find secret comfort in house dresses
reminiscent of those Mom wore to lean out
her warning-window for dinner reminders

the polyester kind never show signs
of opening pickle jars or beer bottles
lace trim frames housework as joyful
from cupboards to carpets to catnaps

few can tell when I pair one with heels
and wear it to work where students
may not recognize a house dress
until projected like a pop-culture skylight

peering over kitchens of sitcom sweeties
and no matter our feminist findings
we miss our hovering TV honeys
who always fixed us a bite to eat

with one-liners ready-to-serve hot or cold
ghetto-gowns glow in city courtyards
lean over laundry lines by Chinese tea houses
in floral patterns of long-gone gardens

grouped by color and hanging wall to wall
in Salvation Armies across America
house dresses wait like surrogate mothers
waving flags of forgiveness for everyone

Zaynab in the Community College Writing Lab

I

she wears a smile and a pink floral dress
her black hijab is laced in gold trim
leather boots   two-inch heels   gold buckles
I help her edit a descriptive essay about a home
her family rented for many years in Iraq
my birth house   my birth house   my birth house

we discuss repetition   choose carefully
my brothers   my brothers   all killed
I sigh softly   continue professionally
postpone empathy for the drive home
*my mother planted jasmine in the yard
the smell filled our house like fairy kisses*

does she know jasmine symbolizes love
represents good luck in some cultures
*my mother always cooked outside until my father
built her a clay oven so she could cook inside
we told jokes at night   counted stars
on the roof where we slept many nights*

Zaynab reads aloud to check her verb tense
voice as maternal as her rings are gold
*in 2017 we returned to my birth house to visit
but a lady turned it into a mosque   I was sad
I hoped to return one day to live in it again
we learned that everything changes   even people*

*but not sunlight that used to fill our living room
my birth house stands forever in my heart*
it has been nearly an hour   she thanks me
smiles goodbye over her shoulder
I imagine her on the big screen at Sundance
another student enters   Vera Bradley backpack

half-empty café mocha   same assignment
my homeland   my homeland   my homeland

II

Zaynab returns in the spring
seemingly surprised I remember her
she is to respond to a work recently read
using stories from her own life

*I read an essay about compassion
the author said one has to suffer
to learn to be compassionate
I agree with this theory because*

she continues the birth house story
*in summer 2004 a bomb landed on the roof
of our home in Iraq where I was sleeping
with my two sisters and four brothers*

she hides her hands into overlong sleeves
as if one parent waits in each
*we were all injured and neighbors jumped
from their rooftops to ours but many died*

she does not appear nervous to share
her memory was merciful
I've done the math
fourteen years have passed

*my mother sent a messenger to our father
he was working when a boy rushed in
to tell him his sons had been killed*
we speak in our softest voices

international laborers of love
raw-material homemakers
inspecting line by line   stone by stone
building   repairing   her structure

Firefighter to Grandchild

> —*After the burning of Notre Dame Cathedral*

can you believe they called them cherry pickers
no not for cherries that night

hose high as hope could hang
along towers and iron gates

we fought those furious flames
faces aglow   red suits covered

in the soot of ages and legends
then   under an evening sky

like a Christmas movie scene we heard
what classic films call villagers

singing hymns under a snow of ash
tiny figures dark   but swaying

Man Made Art

>—*For Archibald MacLeish*

again the voices of yesterday
grant permission to our young

MacLeish heard them all the way home
trekking through blinding snow
to tell Ada things would be different
he would not accept the partnership

a man of letters and *certain* deeds
anyway enough with poetic attorneys

did she embrace her lover of words
a lone gargoyle protecting his goals
as if she could reach so far
despite her own abandoned hope

they crossed the Atlantic to Paris
searching for space and silence

like Toklas and Stein after midnight
Picasso till the light was gone
Fitzgerald at The Dingo *don't go*
Hemingway cornered at Les Deux Magot

Gerald Murphy said it best
only the invented part of life is worth living

Archie befriended bohemian ghosts
calling from centuries-old garden beds
bent his ear toward their haunting
filling basilica halls even now

it's all about masterpieces
and the sound of the Seine is nice too

A Refugee's Ode to Yet

and when asked if she had been
to that horizon in the distance
she said not yet but someday

she would soon share the journey
with yellow-eyed dreamers
forever beholden to yet

a concept slippery but graspable
and when she heard nearby children
ask yet questions in stocking feet

she guarded what was left
of their fleeting innocence
offered fairytale beginnings

she the great predicter of endings
but O the map of our world has changed
whole cultures lost at sea

yet she starts each morning
stacking new skills like pyramids
each yet question a star

wished upon by moonlight
named for the babies of strangers
spared the darkness of never

I Want to Ask My Mother

I want to ask my mother
what exactly my father did
what happened all those years ago
but it will only make her cry
if not at first soon after
does she need another reason
I resort to sorting her jewelry drawer
for the twenty billionth time
untangling sparkly tumbleweeds
remembering what made Dad laugh
what brought him to tears at night
his silhouette at our kitchen table
chain smoke stroking his hair back
I only know he was sent here   there
wherever they send cracked cameos
and if ever there was one
it is hard to imagine individuals
stay in one box for life
I want to ask my mother
but does it matter now
when her mind is on her own flesh
sinking in the palms of her hands
the curve of her pageant-winning neck
I ask if she still needs this key chain
two heart-shaped red-leather cutouts
baseball stitched together at the edges
"Dad made that" she asserts
reminding me of the popsicle stick box
he once wrapped for me
embarrassed yet proud
he made it while recovering   here
there   I filled it years ago
with a few small pieces I gathered

I Heard a Woman

the next caller waited long to get through
if she were her war-torn flag
charred stars would scatter unmarked

I heard a woman whose anguish blazed
red in her throat like a roadside flare
a wailing soon wordless

more music than message
a worry so weary
no setting or dial could silence it

I heard a woman whose plea proved to me
even instrumentals bring listeners to tears
even blank faces   even from here

Squirrel Hill Tunnel

driving through Pittsburgh
reminded my news brain today
that when some leaders speak

tunnels are smart to tune out
of South Lawn broadcasts
for some therapeutic radio silence

I opened my windows to absorb the sound
of my time machine's wheels spinning
lights strobing overhead almost ticking by

like sprocket holes on film strip
I heard centuries of voices this morning
forcing my impatience to focus

on that bright opening straight ahead
as Mother and Father Time must do
through millenniums of toll booths

time zones and tyrannical reruns
when I broke back into daylight
I realized it was only one channel

and they've been lying forever
longer than the lives of iron cities
where neighbors connect regardless

Is Maria There

he was a handsome little boy with a brown bowl cut
and an unusually high voice
but he was in the lowly seventh grade
and I was an adulting eighth grader

we rode the same school bus that year
I wore an older-than-you grin

he never tried to impress or tease like mean city kids
never made fun of my purple paisley pants
or told me my knees were dirty
which I never understood back then

Jeremy joked about *Three's Company*
a good Jack Tripper to my bad Chrissy

come winter we began to pass by his house
he was some sort of seriously sick
by spring he wore a helmet to school
I pretended not to notice   he pretended not to care

he even had the courage to ask my number
and with a mix of worry and pity I gave it

I can still hear him asking for me
before I panicked and hung up
maybe I could pretend wrong number
but Jeremy had been hospitalized

he was calling from there
I'd fashion some silly excuse

by summer I sat in his empty seat scolding myself
thirty years later I drive by the porch stairs
he came bouncing down mornings
all smiles in primary colors

clear as day again *is Maria there*
and I finally answer *this is*

The Wheel

standing mostly backpack at the entrance
unable yet to form his t-h's he greeted
the nice man who held the big door
"Jank you" and into kindergarten he went

school offered friends and discipline and fun
at home I aimed for conversation and comfort
affection and comedy and alone time
in the car I spun Simon and Garfunkel

mostly we listened to NPR and he stared
hard out car windows studying
I filled every hole with explanation
careful as a team of city planners

he learned space and balance and wonder
we drove through Obama and gay rights
Occupy and swine flu and Colorado pot
Rocketman #metoo and Parkland

I answered quick questions
every trip a mobile dinner table
recently he stared as he told me he intends
to become a Marine then paved it with

and someday an engineer addressing
my worries with patience and determination
now he steers and tells *me* everything
with confidence and patience when I'm wrong

which is unusually often I'm learning
I can barely keep up   a trailer in tow
soon he'll be old enough to drive alone
it will take all my resolve to see life

as he does from teenage driveways
he will tell me his plans and I will listen
a good girl studying hard out windows
for space and balance and wonder

Tug of War

*Dumb question but
I know you said this already but
you're all gonna think I'm stupid but
if you're peer reviewing my paper
I apologize ahead of time*

she resembles a young Maya Angelou
fumbles through freshman English
at a community college
in rural Western New York
during the heat of late July

the campus a mile or so
from a small city where
men imagine walls in every direction
women push baby strollers
past drug houses to playgrounds

she stops me in the hall
out of breath before our 8am class
*I hate to bother you but
you may have heard the news
police are looking for a man*

*he murdered someone last night
he's my uncle
I may have to leave early
I might be getting some calls
I'm sorry to bother you*

she is not afraid to get personal
her first essay revealed her roots
humanizing her late father
who fancied himself a musician
singing around her mother's kitchen

the same electric spirit
attracted strange women to his bed
even as his ten children visited
his idea of family time
she could have forgiven him this

had he lived longer than her teens
and she lost her stepfather too
the one who showed her
how to cast a fishing rod
how to have a conversation

her uncle now on the run
I play tug of war with him
I cannot tell her to ignore her phone
but whisper and wink *stay with us
we're just the distraction you need*

she leaves the room twice in three hours
returns quickly each time
knows I see her rope burns
wants to know if she needs to revise
her story that earned her an A

After Attending a Wake for a Man in his Twenties

I did not know the young man who drowned
parents returning home to find their grown son
housesitting face down in their swimming pool

my friend remembers him as that poor boy
with the fireworks sparking up his pants legs
the whole neighborhood heard about it

good family good parents and good and good
any middle-aged person who has lived reasonably
will find themselves facing funeral home driveways

surprisingly often getting to know the routine
you know   walk in and choose which wake it is
like choosing your film in a movie complex

I was hoping the line we saw at the entrance
of the service we attended yesterday
was for the old woman in the picture frame

on the fake cherry wood desk in the lobby
because no one was crying or even quiet
more like a banquet hall in June

his age should have made the difference
don't we save our composure for the old
don't we fall a little apart for the young

but the crowd was for the man not yet thirty
the funeral director asked if everyone was OK
even joked *don't want anyone to keel over waiting*

spurts of laughter followed and my face tightened
I tried not to strike the cell phone out of the hands
of Dude near me scrolling through sports videos

I wanted tears and hugs and grief and stories
and puffy faces and hung heads and then
someone tapped my shoulder and I smiled big too

happy to see an old neighbor hey *how are you
great and you* and what's new and how's whoever
I stood aside watching myself like a furious ghost

after a while I met the victim's calm mother
fought back my tears to not trigger hers
on our way out we passed other processions

where gentlemen removed their good Sunday hats
silence filling the room with remembered conversations
any smiles just polite offerings and many to strangers

I watched them talk outside as we pulled slowly away
they spoke softly as if trained reminding me
of all we learn in our short lives but for the tragedies

A Portrait of Your Boy and Mine

> *After a photo of two boys at a Dominican orphanage—*
> *one young, handicapped, the other, a teen, on a mission trip.*

my son was only told yours was orphaned
and surely you're wondering wherever you are
you do wonder don't you how he's doing

of course and of course you are alive
dear mother and yes it must be far
it must be a long and worrying distance

I wanted to show you your angel so able
and my athlete a gentle and generous soul
at play and hoped somehow you could see

they connected today though mine was unsure
if yours could speak and certainly not English
but sunlight abetted through a golden window

and I know wherever you are dear mother
you are wondering so yes he smiles and see here
he has a bed and a blanket and a pillow all clean

Paying My Way through College

go ahead   squeeze that bottle dry
Schembech would animate twisting his fists
squeeeeze that last drop   riiiight
I learned to have his Black Velvet and chaser
ready as soon as he came hobbling
hip-sore past the front window
in his usual mechanics' navy blue

better use his favorite glass
warned the cook doing life
when he yells the power goes out
I became accustomed to his spit-fights
with fools dumb enough
to news-challenge him
he'd slam his thick glass down

wobbling away still tipping a dollar
to save from embarrassment next time
on holidays he'd pile two singles
with slick pride like Barney Fife
slapping them loudly to be sure
I noticed his not-a-jerk smirk
and so other old-timers would resist

calling him a cheap sonofabitch
I kept busy until the end of my shift
at the mercy of thickly-varnished men
who would otherwise label me lazy
they never had to wait for refills
enjoyed soft rock on the jukebox
songs about sailing and road life

soon regulars would smile toward me
like I was a floor-model television
trusted to help them tune out and relax
I had finally become dear or hon'
a role I would happily play for the chance
to send small checks to the university
leave that place one drop at a time

To the School Shooter

because you have forced me to imagine
I have completed my letter now
I refuse to write it at your choosing
you will not tell me when or how to grieve
first understand that he belongs to me
you belong to unavoidable cycles
beyond rehabilitation just wired that way
you see nothing and nothing sees you back
I know nearly every bite
my boy has ever consumed
carefully crafted every meal
snuck carrots into smoothies
and he grew and grew and grew
even to his own surprise
towering over relatives
learning to lift long legs better into cars
calve muscles finally tone
after years of my bird-leg jokes
ages of athletic determination
years of great job and big boy now
you would stop the growing
but he belongs to me
goodness set in stone
what you wanted for yourself
your problem will not solve
your power is fleeting
it will be your life taken
ours can only be shortened
and though your picture will poison
another impressionable audience
across your television sky
we mothers recognize waste
a temporary blip in the forecast
elements not worth composting
double your pain a hundred million times

and you will still forever miscalculate
the amount of care we plant
you will never be given credit
for choosing to infect a garden
and you will not take our children with you
cut flowers in place of a trophy

Why I Should Never Be Responsible for Another Living Being

he's sixteen and I still can't sleep
what if he's hot   what if he's cold
I'll go cover him up even though
when I open his door the bottom
brushes the carpet making that noise
it'll wake him and it's a school night
he has two comforters but they're twisted
tightly around him like rope   some here
some there   bare skin showing
I'll get another and put it on top
but the only blanket nearby is in a chair
with a half-eaten bag of chips on it
move the chips and I'll startle him silly
I'll turn the heat on   thermostat's right here
but when we turn it on ticking sounds
follow a series of pounds and bangs
like we live above a bowling alley
no one can sleep through that
fine   I'll bring our portable heater in
but that's a potential fire hazard
I'll get a blanket from the bin over there
but the handles click   it'll surely wake him
well   he's sixteen   if he's cold
he can do something about it
back to bed   nice and warm
but it's only 2 a.m. and by 4 he'll be colder
still I force myself back asleep
enter the fish dream   always a tank
half water half filth   too many fish
some dead   in the dark   they look cold
water stale as a half-eaten bag of chips
I hover over wearing my worry face
same old shock in forgetting
I even own a fish tank   and once again
I cannot find the fish food
I cannot find the fish food
I cannot find the fish food

Another Buffalo Banquet

if you park a ten-second walk or less
from the main and only reasonable entrance
to the Italian place known for big portions
you've arrived early having been before
and agreed to the event with kindness
knowing the night will generally go well

if you park alongside the building
you'll bite your lip and tongue as well
during the longer windy walk remembering
the last time you saw the honored guest
reminding yourself you're doing right
earning good karma to boot

if you have to park on the street ah yes
so much for great parking you wonder
*what has this bum ever done for me
I don't even really like him much anyhow*
from what you remember he's cheap as dirt
and the food is probably gone now anyway

suppose you end up next building over
becoming that guy who isn't quite
blocking the driveway *don't be a jerk
there's nowhere else to park you can see*
you're only here because your wife'll be mad
face it   you'll never learn to say no

if you get stuck at the far end of the line
of poor bastards who end up on the street
you're here out of obligation and couldn't
care less about anyone or anything
the sausage better not be boiled and dammit
there better be somewhere near it to sit

if you have no choice but to park around the corner
now you're really mad and will have to be late
don't ever ask me to do this again
if I wanted Italian food I'd order a pizza
and he'll never notice if I show up or not
he owes me a pair of shoes for Chrissakes

and if you can't find a spot at all
you'll cycle through a range of emotions
varying from *he'll never miss me*
to what can you do there's nowhere to park
grab a sub on your short drive home
start the email *please forgive me Good Johnny*

Pre-Caffeine Minutia

our town's favorite coffee and donut place
is named for a Canadian hockey player
however redundant   and I know nothing
of him save that he met an early death
and   I would like to think   liked coffee

today I am grateful for the garbage can
provided in the drive-thru lane
cleaning whatever I can reach this busy AM
while waiting patiently for rations
like medication time at Nurse Ratchet's window

the line in front of me curves like a C
I observe each driver's etiquette
when approaching the large brown bin
which happens to be more interesting
than radio aftermath of the Mueller Report

a blue Chevy owner attempts to dispose
of empty coffee cups by stuffing
one inside the other and when he tries
to push them into the thick flap
one pops out landing behind his front wheel

he wants to drive away but knows
we have all witnessed his misfortune
still he decides to honor his bumper sticker
which shows a stick figure humping
a capital I and lower case t

next is a woman most likely named Susie
who phone-to-ear pushes a paper bag of trash
without touching the must-be-filthy lid
her brown bag rips scattering
a batch of scratch-off tickets

it develops from dawn until dusk
indifferent as a Polaroid
this monument of waste and excess
clean and empty and before for long
heavy with hurry hunger and haste

The Scenery of Saviors

how many times had I driven by
without noticing the ambulance
parked in the firehouse lot

and how many more passes until
I considered its occupants
one gadget-lit   other asleep

can it really be a passing detail
that some await among us
for the wild calls of strangers

please come now   please hurry
and though they never see the endings
of plots they help deliver

they always promise happy ones
I pass through thickening hours
of oppressive summer heat

their vehicle so small compared
to the lot or the nearby field
they land off center in my view

as subjects usually do in poetic shots
like a movie set from the road
credits roll above in a ray of streetlight

the hall itself assertive and watchful
a well-lit fatherly face of protection
over a silent scene

Middle Life

> "What if this is as good as it gets?"
> —Melvin Udall

I'm a city girl living
for longwinded reasons
in a speed-zone suburb

early to my son's game
watching the parallel street
across the baseball field

fifteen miles per hour
between seven and six
on school days

cars crawl single file
like a funeral procession
I find myself laughing

at the lone biker
stuck in the middle
a patient pickle

like me he wonders
if he should or shouldn't
die here

Maria Sebastian is known mostly for her versatility in all things creative. As a musician, she regularly plays classic country and '80s/'90s alternative as well as her own singer/songwriter original music and has opened for dozens of national acts in various genres recording with many of their members. She has also earned over a dozen music awards locally and nationally as well as teaching awards in her area where she is an adjunct professor of English and public speaking in the SUNY system.

In 2011, Maria familiarized herself with the Buffalo poetry community and has since been published in dozens of journals as well as hosting or co-hosting poetry series in her area. "While lyrics are poetic and poems are lyrical, I find them to be difficult to write simultaneously. It's either a poetry season or a song season. I just listen as the stories decide."

Visit mariasebastian.com for more.

www.ingramcontent.com/pod-product-compliance
Lightning Source LLC
LaVergne TN
LVHW041504070426
835507LV00012B/1312